THRIVING
IN THE
Wilderness

A DEVOTIONAL JOURNAL

SARAH K. HOWLEY

Thriving in the Wilderness: A Devotional Journal

Copyright © 2021 Sarah K. Howley

All rights reserved. No part of this publication may be reproduced, distributed, or transmitted in any form or by any means, including photocopying, recording, or other electronic or mechanical methods, without the prior written permission of the author, except in the case of brief quotations and certain other noncommercial uses permitted by copyright law.

Flaming Dove Press, an imprint of
InspiritEncourage LLC
1602 Belle View Blvd #5081
Alexandria, VA 22307
www.inspiritencourage.com

ISBN 978-1-7369071-1-5 (ebook)

ISBN 978-1-7369071-4-6 (print)

Quantity sales. Special discounts are available on quantity purchases by churches, associations, and others. For details, contact the publisher at admin@inspiritencourage.com.

All Bible references are from the New International Version (NIV) unless otherwise noted. Scripture taken from the Holy Bible, NEW INTERNATIONAL VERSION®, NIV® Copyright © 1973, 1978, 1984, 2011 by Biblica, Inc.® Used by permission. All rights reserved worldwide.

Day 6—The Lord Makes a Way in the Wilderness

Forget the former things; do not dwell on the past. See, I am doing a new thing! Now it springs up; do you not perceive it? I am making a way in the wilderness and streams in the wasteland.

Is 43:18-19

Prayer

Lord, I want this to be a time of cleansing. Forgive me my sins [insert specific sins here] and cleanse me from within. Help me carry out forgiveness as you have instructed us. I surrender my pride and my right to revenge; I forgive [name/for offense]. Make me the vessel you have designed me to be, that I may carry your love to others.

Amen.

Reflection

Take time to ask forgiveness for specific sins. If you have a fireplace, you can even write these down and burn them up. If not, then draw fire and depict the sin or write it in the fire of forgiveness.

Consider any sin of unforgiveness that you may carry. Begin the forgiving them by writing,

_____ I forgive you for _____.

The wilderness is a place of reckoning. It is a time to evaluate where we have been and where we are going. It is an opportune time to reflect on any sin that we may be holding on to or continuing in and send it away, as far as the east is from the west. Remember that the Israelites were stuck in the wilderness as punishment for their sin. The scapegoat described in this passage 'atones' or makes amends for the sin of the Israelites. The goat literally carried away the sins of the people and purified them, just as Jesus carried away our sins and purified us. We are blessed to live in the age of Jesus, where such sacrifice is no longer required. However, what is still required is to confess our sin.

We need not hold on to our sins any longer, but God has given us that choice – to hold on or let go of sin. 1 John 1:9 says that if we confess, we are forgiven. We often think of sin as something that we have done against others, but it is first against God. We have gone against his guidance for us. This may be treating others badly or dishonorably, it may be withholding forgiveness, it may be lies we have told, the list is long.

Just as the Israelites put their hands on the head of the goat and then sent it away with their sins, we too much acknowledge our sins that Jesus has already borne. We can then accept the forgiveness assured us in 1 John. Having been forgiven ourselves, our hearts are then in a better place to offer forgiveness to others.

Day 5—The Wilderness is a Place of Forgiveness

But the goat chosen by lot as the scapegoat shall be presented alive before the Lord to be used for making atonement by sending it into the wilderness as a scapegoat. The goat will carry on itself all their sins to a remote place; and the man shall release it in the wilderness.

Leviticus 16:10, 22

Prayer

Lord, you are the great *I am*. Reveal yourself to me in this deserted place where I find myself. You say if I seek you, I will find you. Reveal yourself to me.

Amen.

Reflection

God has many names in the Bible. Choose one or two that are most relevant in this wilderness and meditate upon them. Make an acrostic of the name, with each letter of the name used in a characteristic of God. For example, take the word LORD: Love Omnipotent Real wisDom (If we followed the rules strictly then I would say *Dear* for the last letter, but let worshiping and knowing God be more important than rules!).

The Lord reveals himself in the wilderness. The Lord set a bush aflame without burning, just to catch Moses's attention. This is the same encounter when God says who he is, *I am* and the God of Abraham, Isaac, and Jacob. He reveals who he is: He is our God.

Day 4—The Lord Reveals Himself in the Wilderness

Now Moses was tending the flock of Jethro his father-in-law, the priest of Midian, and he led the flock to the far side of the wilderness and came to Horeb, the mountain of God. There the angel of the LORD appeared to him in flames of fire from within a bush. Moses saw that though the bush was on fire it did not burn up. So Moses thought, "I will go over and see this strange sight—why the bush does not burn up." When the LORD saw that he had gone over to look, God called to him from within the bush, "Moses! Moses!"

And Moses said, "Here I am."

Exodus 3:1-4

Prayer

Lord, I do believe; help me overcome my unbelief! (Mark 9:24) Grow that mustard seed of faith in me, that I may stand strong in you. Teach me to slay the giants one step at a time.

Amen.

Reflection

The wilderness can be a place of preparation for the slaying of giants yet to come. Do you have the faith of our ancestors (Hebrews 11)? Take time to review those listed in Hebrews 11 and note the actions that demonstrated their faith.

We know David as a young man in this scene. He raised sheep in the wilderness, where he has fought off the various predators of the flock. The time in the wilderness has prepared him to face off with this new giant, the enemy of Israel. The wilderness has given David confidence in God, has deepened his faith. David is now prepared to fight off the giants. You are in the same place David was, one of preparation.

This time in the wilderness will prepare you by deepening your faith, growing your confidence in God. *You* may feel unprepared to fend off the lions and bears, but remember the purpose is to grow your confidence in God, not yourself. This wilderness can encourage your faith and build trust in the mighty One. Whatever has brought you here, **nothing** is too hard for God.

Day 3 – The Wilderness is a Place of Preparation for Slaying Giants

Early in the morning David left the flock in the care of a shepherd, loaded up and set out, as Jesse had directed. He reached the camp as the army was going out to its battle positions, shouting the war cry.

But David said to Saul, "Your servant has been keeping his father's sheep. When a lion or a bear came and carried off a sheep from the flock, I went after it, struck it and rescued the sheep from its mouth. When it turned on me, I seized it by its hair, struck it and killed it. Your servant has killed both the lion and the bear; this uncircumcised Philistine will be like one of them, because he has defied the armies of the living God. The LORD who rescued me from the paw of the lion and the paw of the bear will rescue me from the hand of this Philistine."

1 Samuel 17:20, 34-37

Prayer

Holy Spirit, I cannot pass through this season without you. Make your presence known and felt within me. Accompany me. Send others to hold me up and encourage me and demonstrate your love to me.

Amen.

Reflection

In looking back on this time since the wilderness began, do you see evidence of the presence of the Spirit? How has the Holy Spirit been accompanying you on this journey?

Who else has joined you, lifted you up, encouraged you, or prayed for you on this journey? If you have not shared that you are walking in the wilderness at this time, talk with a friend about it. You are not alone because the Spirit is with you. Yet the Spirit lives in others as well, ready to comfort you and counsel you through them. Reach out if you have not yet. If you have reached out, thank them for listening, accompanying you, and holding you in prayer.

It is easy to mistake the wilderness as punishment, but it is not automatically so. Jesus, who was without sin, also spent time in the wilderness. So, we can hold fast to Jesus, who sinned not, knowing that he was *sent* by the Spirit to the wilderness. What better reason to be in this place than to be sent by the Spirit!

We can be certain that if the Spirit sends us, we are also accompanied by him. The Holy Spirit is perhaps best known as the Comforter and Counselor. Be assured that you are held in the arms of the Comforter in this time; lean on him. The Spirit is also Counselor and leads you through this time. Listen well so that you are ready to hear and feel the Spirit.

Day 2–The Holy Spirit Accompanies Me

Jesus, full of the Holy Spirit, left the Jordan and was led by the Spirit into the wilderness, where for forty days he was tempted by the devil. He ate nothing during those days, and at the end of them he was hungry.

Luke 4:1-2

Prayer

Lord, I cannot wait to see the splendor of your glory. Take this fear from me, strengthen my feeble hands, and steady my knees. You are my strength and my joy; I praise you.

Amen.

Reflection

Hope can be defined as a future expectation of good because of faith in God. What is your hope as you pass through this season in the wilderness?

The last verse says to 'be strong, do not fear;' what do you fear about this season?

The wilderness looks like empty wasteland where we find little surrounding us. But this land is under God's rule, and it will be filled with life and the splendor of God's glory in due time. The difficulty of the wilderness is that it is empty. But we are only graced with sight for this world and not the next. But God can see the trees and the crocus that he has already planted in this place. He knows when they will bloom and grow, adding color and brightness to your day.

This is the hope we have: that this season will end. This season in the wilderness may last a few weeks; it may last several months or even years. But the hope remains that it is temporary. The end of the wilderness will come, in this life or the next. God has promised that we are not alone, and indeed this passage from Isaiah encourages us to be strong and urges us not to fear. The acknowledgment of God's strength follows that. He is mighty to save and mighty to alter the wilderness and make it bloom. God is already working in your circumstances to bring you forth in victory.

Day 1—This Season is Temporary

The desert and the parched land will be glad; the wilderness will rejoice and blossom. Like the crocus, it will burst into bloom; it will rejoice greatly and shout for joy. The glory of Lebanon will be given to it, the splendor of Carmel and Sharon; they will see the glory of the Lord, the splendor of our God. Strengthen the feeble hands, steady the knees that give way; say to those with fearful hearts, "Be strong, do not fear; your God will come, he will come with vengeance; with divine retribution he will come to save you."

Isaiah 35: 1-4

Know that 'The Lord himself goes before you and will be with you; he will never leave you nor forsake you. Do not be afraid; do not be discouraged,' (Deuteronomy 3:18) as you learn to thrive in the wilderness.

Feel free to send me your feedback. I'd love to hear from you.

Sarah

Introduction

The Lord himself goes before you and will be with you; he will never leave you nor forsake you. Do not be afraid; do not be discouraged.

Deuteronomy 3:18

When we find ourselves in the midst of struggles or storms and deserted in a wasteland, it is then that we drop to our knees and cry out to God. We want to know why or what is going on. But rarely do we receive the answer while we walk through the wasteland.

So, we pass through it. It is not easy, and we must look hard for water and nourishment. This devotional is designed to help us find the oasis that is our God and cling to him in the wasteland. In knowing Him more deeply, seeking Him evermore, our victory is found in Him as we pass through the season of wilderness thriving instead of surviving.

This 10-day prayer journal and devotional is laid out with a passage of scripture, then a few comments on the wilderness and how God uses it or speaks to us through it. And I've included reflections each day of this journey; some reflections are thought-provoking, and others may push you out of your comfort zone into art or poetry. Use the space provided in the prayer area to draw or write out prayers for the day.

Table of Contents

Introduction 1

Day 1—This Season is Temporary 4

Day 2—The Holy Spirit Accompanies Me 8

Day 3 - The Wilderness is a Place of Preparation for
Slaying Giants 12

Day 4—The Lord Reveals Himself in the Wilderness......... 16

Day 5—The Wilderness is a Place of Forgiveness 20

Day 6—The Lord Makes a Way in the Wilderness............ 24

Day 7—The Wilderness is a Place of Feasting 28

Day 8—He Refreshes Our Soul in the Wilderness............. 32

Day 9—God Works Solutions in the Wilderness 36

Day 10—The Word Becomes Real in the Wilderness........ 40

Acknowledgments 44

About the Author 46

The Lord is doing a new thing. Anything is possible. The past is just that—the past. He wants to make us new and do new things in us. The wilderness is the perfect opportunity for us to grow more like Jesus through the power of the Holy Spirit in us. That will make us new. That will change our relationships. That will change our outlook. That will make all things new. He makes all things new.

You may be in a place where things never seem to change. Every week may look just like the week before. Struggle and hardship have perhaps become the norm. But God makes all things new. He sees what is coming, and that starts with you. He sees you made into the image of his son. The new you will see the same old life through new eyes.

Reflection

Are you willing to participate in this new thing? Write a simple prayer of your concerns to God.

What new thing do you desire God to do?

Prayer

Lord, you are doing a new thing and making a way in this wilderness where I find myself. Show me this new thing that you are doing, reveal it to me that I may advance your will in me.

Amen.

Day 7—The Wilderness is a Place of Feasting

Afterward Moses and Aaron went to Pharaoh and said, "This is what the Lord, the God of Israel, says: 'Let my people go, so that they may hold a festival to me in the wilderness.'"

Exodus 5:1

The wilderness is a place of feasting and celebration. The Israelites went to the wilderness to worship and hold a festival for God. God is God all the time. He is good. He is great and worthy of praise. By praising and thanking God, we raise him out of this earthly plain and exalt his mighty power and everlasting love. We make him the focus of our days and nights rather than making the wilderness our focus. Just as Peter sank in the water when he looked at his circumstances but was saved when he focused on Jesus, we must focus on Jesus. He will carry us through this wilderness. Perhaps we don't celebrate God enough, but the wilderness is a great time to start.

Reflection

Take time to praise God. Turn on some music if that helps and sing along. Make a list of the good things that God has done in your life to remind you how He is worthy of praise.

Make a list of people you are thankful to God for. Then add things that you are thankful for. Consider writing a gratefulness journal of just one line a day.

Prayer

Lord, I praise you. You are indeed worthy of praise; you are faithful and loving. You have done great things for me [include your above list]. Thank you for all the care you have for me. I have faith you are working in the wilderness with me and in me. I will have even more reason to praise you soon, very soon.

Amen.

Day 8—He Refreshes Our Soul in the Wilderness

While he [Elijah] himself went a day's journey into the wilderness. He came to a broom bush, sat down under it and prayed that he might die. "I have had enough, LORD," he said. "Take my life; I am no better than my ancestors." Then he lay down under the bush and fell asleep. All at once an angel touched him and said, "Get up and eat." He looked around, and there by his head was some bread baked over hot coals, and a jar of water. He ate and drank and then lay down again.

1 Kings 19:4-6

The weariness and depression that we feel in the wilderness are not unusual. This passage from 1 Kings shows that the prophet Elijah sat down and prayed he would die. Our situations and circumstances here on earth can be dire, scary, and overwhelming. God sees your needs. He knows your emotions and felt them himself through the life of Jesus. He too experienced sadness, separation, loneliness, heartbreak, grief; He experienced every emotion that you and I do. He knows our needs. He will provide the rest and nourishment necessary to continue on, just as he did for Elijah.

Reflection

In this season, are you weary or depressed? What emotion are you feeling most deeply? Look up verses that address that need and note them here. His word fills us with His Spirit and meets our spiritual needs.

Carve time out to do something refreshing: a walk in the park, painting class, visit a rock-climbing gym, call a friend or whatever treat makes you feel God's presence. Nature, creating, fellowship, worship are all ways to refresh our souls.

Prayer

Lord, I am weary, alone, depressed, [list your feelings with honesty]. Shower me with your delight and lift me from this darkness. Nourish me and give me rest.

Amen.

Day 9—God Works Solutions in the Wilderness

While Aaron was speaking to the whole Israelite community, they looked toward the desert, and there was the glory of the LORD appearing in the cloud. The LORD said to Moses, "I have heard the grumbling of the Israelites. Tell them, 'At twilight you will eat meat, and in the morning you will be filled with bread. Then you will know that I am the LORD your God.'" That evening quail came and covered the camp, and in the morning there was a layer of dew around the camp. When the dew was gone, thin flakes like frost on the ground appeared on the desert floor.

Exodus 16:10-14

We have difficulty seeing a solution in the wilderness. God, the creator of the universe, doesn't just *find* a solution. He **makes** solutions. God is *the* Creator. Quail and the manna came from heaven, they were not an earthly solution. God provides, even in the wilderness. God is not limited by *our* imagination; his imagination is much greater than ours. Consider nature, the giraffe, or the platypus, the touch-me-not fern, or the Venus flytrap; they show God is wise and lord of all. God's solutions are not limited to what we can see or think.

Reflection

Has the Lord heard your cries? Describe your circumstances and outline the solution you desire, but trust the solution to Him, let His will be done.

If the problem can be represented by something physical, like a building, then go there are do a prayer walk. Walk around the place and invite God to work the solution.

Prayer

Lord, in the wilderness, you sent manna and quail to solve an impossible problem, a *seemingly* impossible problem. Look at this problem, Lord [pour out your problems to Him and tell him your complaints]. I can't see a way to solve this; I simply can't see it. But you are the Creator of the universe, and you create; you don't have to see or find. I give this to your hands and ask you to work a solution. Help me have faith that you know and do best, that I may leave this in your hands.

Amen.

Day 10—The Word Becomes Real in the Wilderness

In those days John the Baptist came, preaching in the wilderness of Judea.

Matthew 3:1

The wilderness will open our eyes to the word. The word has a rich and deep meaning that grows when under duress. The wilderness can open our eyes to the word like the pressure of the earth makes a diamond. The Word is the only offensive piece of the armor we are told to wear in Ephesians 6:10-17. The word is our strategy and method of attack. Of course, it is a choice to open and daily read the Bible, choose to make a habit of knowing the Word. Reading the Word and knowing it, letting it infiltrate our core being, are different. The Word may be studied, but without revelation from the Spirit, it will remain empty.

When we are in the wilderness, there are fewer distractions, the barrenness becomes a blessing. That is how I picture John the Baptist, in a barren place where people could hear the word and the Spirit could move. There were few people who were critical of revelation, and there were no noises that distracted from the message. There was only the word; and people heard it, and the Spirit moved.

Reflection

Take time to make some signs or verse art with the verses that most speak to you or encourage you in this season. Place them in conspicuous places around the house, like your key ring, bathroom mirror, closet, or refrigerator door. Memorize these verses as the Word is the only armor of God that is offensive- the sword. Note the verses in this space.

Read Ephesians 6:10-17 and note the armor we wear as believers. If something needs to be repaired or reinforced before heading into battle, the wilderness is the place of preparation. Take the time to seek the Word for what you need, be it faith, peace, or other parts of the armor.

Prayer

Lord, thank you for this time in the wilderness where you open my eyes to the word, develop the depth and the breadth of my understanding. Show me how to wield the sword in the fight against the enemy.

Amen.

Acknowledgments

Thank you to my Lord and Savior Jesus Christ for His redeeming work and guidance in writing this short devotional.

Thank you to my family and friends, and especially my husband, who have supported and encouraged me in all the writing I do.

Thank you, readers, for choosing this resource to accompany you in the wilderness. If you liked this book, please check out my site, https://www.inspiritencourage.com, for more Christian encouragement. I love to hear from readers, so please reach out.

To receive notices of Sarah's upcoming books, sign up at https://www.inspiritencourage.com/book-readers-subscribe

Was this book helpful? Did you get something from it? Please visit Amazon or Goodreads and leave a review of this book. Every review makes this book more visible to others.
https://www.amazon.com/review/create-review?asin=B0982PZZT1

To join Sarah's advance reader group, sign up here
https://www.subscribepage.com/flamingdovearc

Christian Books in Multiple Genres, Join Christian Indie Author ~ Readers Group on Facebook. Opportunities to learn more great Christian authors.
https://www.facebook.com/groups/291215317668431/

About the Author

Sarah K. Howley is an author of Christian nonfiction for women. Her first book is titled *Alive Again: Find Healing in Forgiveness.* Sarah is a certified Christian counselor and holds a master's degree in education but prefers the authority of her Bible over those pieces of paper. She was born in Houston, Texas, and has lived on four continents. When not writing at inspiritencourage.com, you can find her eating dark chocolate, sipping soda water, reading, or planning her next trip.

You can find Sarah on Instagram or Facebook @inspiritencourage.

Also by Sarah K. Howley

Non-fiction

Alive Again: Find Healing in Forgiveness

Bible Study

I Am: The Son Reveals the Father by Name

To receive notices of Sarah's upcoming books, sign up at https://www.inspiritencourage.com/book-readers-subscribe

www.ingramcontent.com/pod-product-compliance
Lightning Source LLC
Chambersburg PA
CBHW072210100526
44589CB00015B/2457